N ok

withdrawn

An associate College of the University of Kent

Oxford University Press

Oxford University Press, Walton Street, Oxford OX2 6DP

Oxford   New York   Toronto
Delhi   Bombay   Calcutta   Madras   Karachi
Kuala Lumpur   Singapore   Hong Kong   Tokyo
Nairobi   Dar es Salaam   Cape Town
Melbourne   Auckland   Madrid

and associated companies in
Berlin   Ibadan

Oxford is a trade mark of Oxford University Press

First published as *The Oxford 123 Book of Number Rhymes* 1992
Redesigned edition 1994
1 3 5 7 9 10 8 6 4 2

British Library Cataloguing in Publication Data
Data available

ISBN 0 19 910329 1 (paperback)

Printed in Belgium

Parents' notes

Small children always enjoy simple number rhymes and games, and these provide excellent preparation for number work once school begins. *My Oxford 1 2 3 Number Rhyme Book* is divided into two sections to develop different aspects of counting.

In the first section we have collected together traditional and modern rhymes and songs dealing with the numbers from 1 to 10, along with counting jokes and quizzes, and number friezes. The rest of the book is devoted to rhymes that introduce children to counting in sequence.

You may have to help with the reading or singing of these rhymes to begin with, but your child will soon start to join in. Children learn best when they are having fun. So, if you both see this book as something to enjoy, the learning can safely be left to look after itself.

Nicholas Tucker

1 2 3 4 5 6 7 8 9 10

The one and only. One.
One single and alone.
Is it lonely? Is it proud?
Standing on its own.

Roger McGough

Diddle diddle dumpling my son John,
Went to bed with his trousers on,
One shoe off and one shoe on,
Diddle diddle dumpling my son John.

Hickory dickory dock
The mouse ran up the clock.
The clock struck one;
The mouse ran down,
Hickory dickory dock.

One old orang-utan observing the open ocean.

Can you find all of these?

1 crab
1 sandcastle
1 spade
1 bucket
1 beachball

What did the big hand say to the little hand?

I'll be back in one hour.

one-man band

one-piece

1 2 3 4 5 6 7 8 9 10

Two swans a-swimming
In the warm summer air.
Up the river, down the river,
2 is company. 2 is a pair.

Roger McGough

Two little boats are on the sea,
All is calm as calm can be.
Gently the wind begins to blow,
Two little boats rock to and fro.
Loudly the wind begins to shout,
Two little boats are tossed about.
Gone is the wind, the storm, the rain,
Two little boats sail on again.

Two little eyes to look around,
Two little ears to hear each sound;
One little nose to smell what's sweet,
One little mouth that likes to eat.

Two tiny teddy bears tasting treacle tarts at tea time.

Can you find these pairs?

salt and pepper
oranges and lemons
strawberries and cream

bread and butter
fish and chips
beans and toast

two-seater

Why did the elephant take two trunks on holiday?

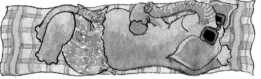

One to drink with, the other to swim in.

two by two

1 2 3 4 5 6 7 8 9 10

Three is a crowd.(But only just.)
I'll tell you a secret if I must.
When I open my eyes what do I see?
Three is Teddy, Bunny and me.

Roger McGough

Three little ghosties
Sitting on three posties
Eating buttered toasties
Sucking their fisties
Right up to their wristies
Weren't they little beasties?

Wire, briar, limber, lock;
Three geese in a flock.
One flew east,
One flew west,
And one flew over
     the cuckoo's nest.

Three thirsty thrushes threading through the thistles.

How many parcels are in the postbox?
How many birds are in the tree?
How many dogs are in the street?
How many children are playing?
How many dustbins can you see?

three-legged race

Have you heard the story of the three wells?

Well, well, well.

three-wheeler

1 2 3 4 5 6 7 8 9 10

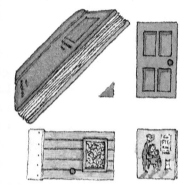

Four corners on a book,
Four corners on the door.
Oh so neat and tidy
(How many letters make fo-u-r?)

Roger McGough

This morning I counted to four:
When the cat jumped on my bed,
1, 2, 3, 4 legs;
When I had my breakfast,
1, 2, 3, 4 chairs;
When I played with my truck,
1, 2, 3, 4 wheels;
And when I had my sleep,
1, 2, 3, 4 . . . .

Four scarlet berries
Left upon the tree.
'Thanks,' said the blackbird,
'These will do for me.'
She ate numbers one and two,
Then ate number three;
When she'd eaten number four,
There was none to see!

Four fat floppy frogs flipping from the freezing fountain.

Can you find all of these?

- 4 furry toys
- 4 toys with wheels
- 4 noisy toys
- 4 toys you would like to play with

four-leaved clover

What has four legs and can't walk?

A bed.

going on all fours

1 2 3 4 5 6 7 8 9 10

Five is your hands favourite number,
Count each finger on your nose.
If that was easy, lift your foot
And try again with your toes.

Roger McGough

Five little monkeys walked along the shore;
One went a-sailing,
Then there were four.

Four little monkeys climbed up a tree;
One of them tumbled down,
Then there were three.

Three little monkeys found a pot of glue;
One got stuck in it,
Then there were two.

Two little monkeys found a currant bun;
One ran away with it,
Then there was one.

One little monkey cried all afternoon,
So they put him in an aeroplane
And sent him to the moon.

Five little squirrels sat up in a tree,
The first one said, 'What do I see?'
The second one said, 'A man with a gun.'
The third one said, 'Then we'd better run.'
The fourth one said, 'Let's hide in the shade.'
The fifth one said, 'I'm not afraid.'
Then **bang** went the gun, and how they did run.

Five furry fox cubs fearlessly frisking through fields and forests.

These five animal babies are looking for their mothers. Can you see where each one should go?

five senses

seeing

hearing

brezzzz

smelling

tasting

touching

What do you call five bottles of lemonade?

A pop group.

1 2 3 4 5 6 7 8 9 10

Six hisses like a serpent,
Six kisses mean a lot.
A yoyo dancing on a string
Trick cyclist balancing on the spot.

Roger McGough

Six little mice sat down to spin,
Pussy passed by, and she peeped in.
'What are you doing, my little men?'
'Weaving coats for gentlemen.'
'May I come in, and cut off your threads?'
'Oh no, Mistress Pussy, you'll bite off our heads!'
'Oh no, I'll not. I'll help you to spin.'
'That may be so, but you can't come in.'

Insects have six legs, no more,
But nobody is really sure
That all those legs are legs not arms.

Maybe they have three of each,
Or four and two, or two and four.

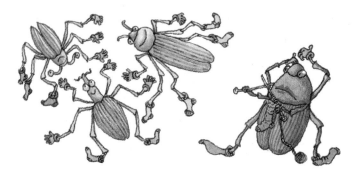

No, nobody is really sure,
When knitting socks for insects.

Six shaggy sheep scampering skilfully in scarlet socks.

These children do not know how to behave in the countryside. Can you see six things they are doing wrong?

1 dropping litter
2 leaving the gate open
3 picking wild flowers
4 chasing the animals
5 stealing birds' eggs
6 lighting a fire

When does a horse have six legs?

When it's got a rider on its back.

six of hearts

half a dozen eggs

1 2 3 4 5 6 7 8 9 10

Seven points the way ahead,
Like a policeman, arm out straight.
Gives direction, sharp and sensible,
Unlike its neighbour, number eight.

Roger McGough

As I was going to St Ives,
I met a man with seven wives.
Each wife had seven sacks,
Each sack had seven cats,
Each cat had seven kits,
Kits, cats, sacks and wives,
How many were going to St Ives?

One - yourself!

I saw seven magpies in a tree

Two for you and five for me:

One for sorrow, two for joy,

Three for a girl, and four for a boy;

Five for silver, six for gold,

shhhhhhh . . . . . .

Seven for a secret never to be told.

Seven skipping schoolchildren singing silly songs.

Can you find seven things these children are doing at school?

1 painting
2 reading
3 writing
4 cutting out
5 modelling
6 measuring
7 singing

seven days of the week

What is furry and has fourteen legs?

Seven teddy bears.

1 2 3 4 5 6 7 8 9 10

Eight is a fat cat. Balancing doughnuts.
A pair of goggles on its side.
A figure of eight a roller coaster
Take your finger for a ride.

Roger McGough

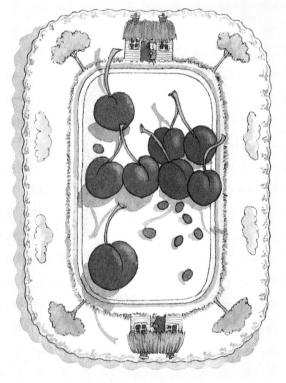

One, two, three, four,
Mary at the cottage door.
Five, six, seven, eight,
Eating cherries off a plate.

Eight babies laughing loud, eight babies singing.

Seven babies clapping hands, one baby ringing.

Six babies banging drums, two babies rattling.

Five babies dancing high, three babies chattering.

Four babies drinking juice, four babies feeding.

Eight babies ready for bed, eight babies sleeping.

Eight excited elephants enjoying an expedition.

Can you spot these eight animals?

parrot   anteater
monkey   bat
toucan   sloth
snake   lizard

figure of eight

What eight-letter word has only one letter in it?

An envelope.

Henry VIII

1 2 3 4 5 6 7 8 9 10

Nine walks tall, puffs out its chest.
Happily banging a big bass drum.
Can you count how many times?
Tum-pity. Tum-pity. Tum, Tum, Tum.

Roger McGough

Pease porridge hot,
Pease porridge cold,
Pease porridge in the pot,
Nine days old.
Some like it hot,
Some like it cold,
Some like it in the pot,
Nine days old.

I'll sing you a song,
Nine verses long,
For a pin:
Three and three are six
And three are nine;
You are a fool,
And the pin is mine.

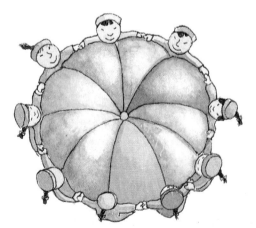

Nine nesting nightingales nibbling nuts in the nippy New Year.

There are nine snowflakes hidden in this picture. Can you find them?

ninepins

If I had four snowballs in my right hand and five in my left, what would I have?

99 ice-cream

Cold hands.

1 2 3 4 5 6 7 8 9

Ten looks really grown-up
(One at last has found a friend)
Ten has lots of tricks to show you
For numbers are fun without end.

Roger McGough

Ten little teddy bears stand up straight,

Ten little teddy bears make a gate,

Ten little teddy bears make a ring,

Ten little teddy bears bow to the king.

Ten little teddy bears dance all day,

Ten little teddy bears hide away.

Cluck, cluck, cluck, cluck.
Good morning, Mrs Hen.
How many chicks have you got?
Madam, I've got ten,
Four of them are yellow,
Four of them are brown,
And two of them are speckled red,
The nicest in the town.

Ten turquoise teapots teetering on the tray.

Mrs Harris went to Paris.
She bought a [hat], an [orange], a [necklace], a [teapot], a [ring], a [brush], a [banana], an [umbrella], a [cake] and a [motorcycle].

How many things did Mrs Harris buy?

ten fingers

If Mrs Harris cuts her orange into four pieces and her banana into six pieces, what will she get?

ten toes

Fruit salad.

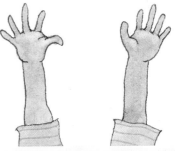

One, two, three,
Mother caught a flea.
Put it in the teapot,
And made a cup of tea.

One, two, three, four, five,
Once I caught a fish alive.
Six, seven, eight, nine, ten,
Then I let it go again.

Why did I let it go?
Because it bit my finger so.
Which finger did it bite?
This little finger on my right.

This old man, he played one,
He played nick-nack on my drum.

With a nick-nack, paddy wack,
Give a dog a bone.
This old man went rolling home.

This old man, he played two,
He played nick-nack on my shoe.

With a nick-nack, paddy wack . . .

This old man, he played three,
He played nick-nack on my knee.

This old man, he played four,
He played nick-nack on my door.

This old man, he played five,
He played nick-nack on my hive.

This old man, he played six,
He played nick-nack on my sticks.

This old man, he played seven,
He played nick-nack up in heaven.

This old man, he played eight,
He played nick-nack on my gate.

This old man, he played nine,
He played nick-nack on my line.

This old man, he played ten,
He played nick-nack on my hen.

The animals went in one by one,
The elephant chewing a caraway bun.

The animals went in two by two,
The rhinoceros and the kangaroo.

The animals went in three by three,
The wasp, the flea and the bumble bee.

The animals went in four by four,
The great hippopotamus stuck in the door.

The animals went in five by five,
With great big trunks they did arrive.

The animals went in six by six,
The hyena laughed at the monkeys' tricks.

The animals went in seven by seven,
Said the ant to the elephant, 'Who are you shoving?'

The animals went in eight by eight,
The worm was early, the bird was late.

The animals went in nine by nine,
Some had water and some had wine.

The animals went in ten by ten,
If you want any more you must sing it again.
And they all went into the Ark,
For to get out of the rain.

One, two,
Buckle my shoe.
Three, four,
Knock at the door.
Five, six,
Pick up sticks.
Seven, eight,
Lay them straight.
Nine, ten,
A big fat hen.
Eleven, twelve,
Dig and delve.
Thirteen, fourteen,
Maids a-courting.
Fifteen, sixteen,
Maids in the kitchen.
Seventeen, eighteen,
Maids in waiting.
Nineteen, twenty,
My plate's empty.

One, two, kittens that mew,
Two, three, birds on a tree,
Three, four, shells on the shore,
Four, five, bees in the hive,
Five, six, the cow that licks,
Six, seven, rooks in the heaven,
Seven, eight, sheep at the gate,
Eight, nine, clothes on the line,
Nine, ten, the little black hen.

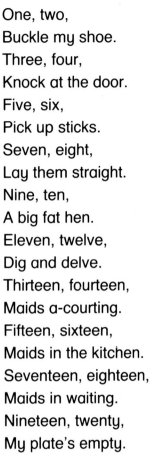

On the first day of Christmas
My true love sent to me
A partridge in a pear tree.

On the second day of Christmas
My true love sent to me
Two turtle doves and
A partridge in a pear tree.

On the third day of Christmas
My true love sent to me
Three French hens . . .

On the fourth day of Christmas
My true love sent to me
Four calling birds . . .

On the fifth day of Christmas
My true love sent to me
Five gold rings . . .

On the sixth day of Christmas
My true love sent to me
Six geese a-laying . . .

On the seventh day of Christmas
My true love sent to me
Seven swans a-swimming...

On the eighth day of Christmas
My true love sent to me
Eight maids a-milking...

On the ninth day of Christmas
My true love sent to me
Nine drummers drumming...

On the tenth day of Christmas
My true love sent to me
Ten pipers piping...

On the eleventh day of Christmas
My true love sent to me
Eleven ladies dancing...

On the twelfth day of Christmas
My true love sent to me
Twelve lords a-leaping...

Ten green bottles standing on the wall,
Ten green bottles standing on the wall,
And if one green bottle should accidentally fall
There'd be nine green bottles standing on the wall.

Nine green bottles standing on the wall,
… (continue)

Eight green bottles standing on the wall …

Seven green bottles standing on the wall …

Six green bottles standing on the wall …

Five green bottles standing on the wall …

Four green bottles standing on the wall …

Three green bottles standing on the wall …

Two green bottles standing on the wall …

One green bottle standing on the wall,
One green bottle standing on the wall,
And if that green bottle should accidentally fall
There'd be no green bottles standing on the wall.

One man went to mow,
Went to mow a meadow;
One man and his dog,
Went to mow a meadow.

Two men went to mow,
Went to mow a meadow;
Two men, one man and his dog,
Went to mow a meadow.

Three men went to mow,
… (continue)

Four men went to mow …

Five men went to mow …

Six men went to mow …

Seven men went to mow …

Eight men went to mow …

Nine men went to mow …

Ten men went to mow …

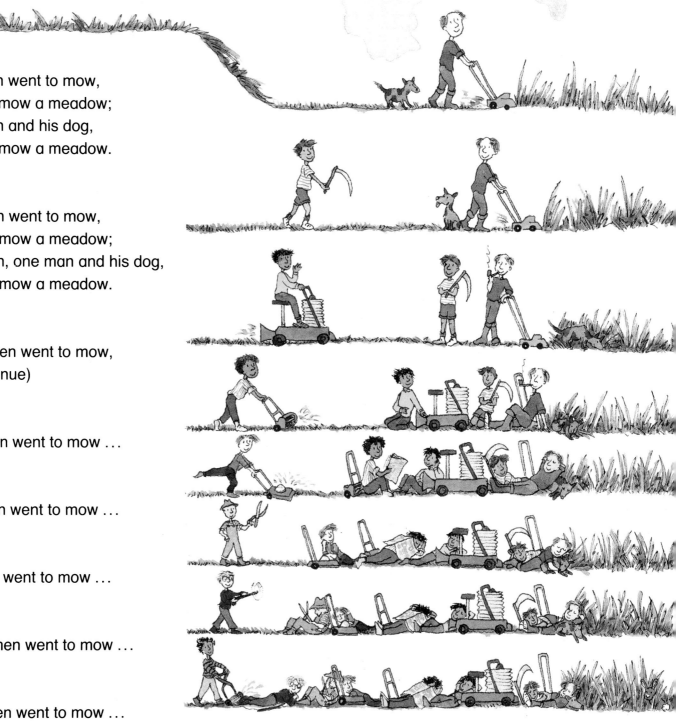

How many animals are there in each of these groups?
See if you can count them for yourself.